Association for Middle Level Educ

Middle Level Leadership

# THE MARK OF
# LEADERSHIP

Strategies for Leading with
Purpose, Plans, and Passion

## Tom Burton

Printed in the United States of America.

ISBN: 978-1-56090-268-3

---

Library of Congress Cataloging-in-Publication Data

Burton, Tom.
  Mark of leadership : leading with purpose, plans, and passion / Tom Burton Association for Middle Level Education.
    pages cm. -- (Middle level leadership)
  Includes bibliographical references and index.
  ISBN 978-1-56090-268-3 (alk. paper)
  1. Middle school education--United States. 2. Middle school teachers--United States. 3. Middle school teaching--United States. 4. Educational leadership--United States.  I. Title.
  LB1623.5.B87 2014
  373.236--dc23
                          2014015039

**Association for Middle Level Education**
4151 Executive Parkway, Suite 300
Westerville, Ohio 43081 | www.amle.org

## Dedication

To my mother and father, who worked tirelessly with students of all
ages showing my sisters and me the importance of giving to others.
Additionally, they showed us the value of love and understanding,
supporting us to follow our dreams. And to my sisters Sally and Betsy,
and Aunt Mary for unyielding support, trust, and friendship. To my wife
Franca, daughter Cailey, and sons Bryce and Tommy for being patient with
me on my journey and loving me all the way. Lastly, to the Ohio Middle
Level Association Executive Board both past and present, Dr. Brian Freidt,
Bill Porter, and countless other staff members, students, friends, and family
members for their help and support.

# Preface

When I was in middle school, my mother would find solace in walking the sandy beaches of Lake Erie and searching for sea glass. Pieces of broken bottles that had been tossed around for who knows how long, those polished gems of sea glass ultimately ended up washing ashore. Noting that she had collected thousands of remnants, I asked my mom why she continued to pick up sea glass and she said, "I think every piece is beautiful—look at this one, I don't have any that are like it." She continued, finding beautiful piece after beautiful piece, and the collection grew.

One day, when I was a young middle grades teacher, it occurred to me that middle school students are like pieces of sea glass. Sometimes they feel discarded, tossed around during the day following hectic schedules, slammed against the floors of the school, wondering when they will finally wash ashore. However, as great teachers and leaders focused on true middle grades practices, we will recognize the sea glass in the sand and polish even the most hardened glass into a beautiful gem.

Apple founder Steve Jobs has a quote intended to highlight difference-makers in our world, but the quote so aptly fits the potential of middle school students we are trying to shape:

> *Here's to the crazy ones—the misfits, the rebels, the troublemakers, the round pegs in the square holes. The ones who see things differently—they're not fond of rules. You can quote them, disagree with them, glorify or vilify them, but the only thing you can't do is ignore them because they change things. They push the human race forward, and while some may see them as the crazy ones, we see genius, because the ones who are crazy enough to think that they can change the world, are the ones who do.*

This book is a collection of columns I wrote for the Association for Middle Level Education's *Middle Ground* magazine. I hope they will inspire you to look for the very best in each of the young adolescents and the staff that you lead on a daily basis and to meet their needs so they become the people who change the world.

# TABLE OF
# CONTENTS

# PLANNING

## *Deciding Your Purpose*

Don't say you don't have enough time. You have exactly the same number of hours per day that were given to Helen Keller, Louis Pasteur, Michelangelo, Mother Teresa, Leonardo da Vinci, Thomas Jefferson, and Albert Einstein.

**—Jackson Browne, Jr., singer**

As a novice middle grades teacher, my revelation came at the end of that first year. As the last student left the building, I was swept with emotions. That's it? It's over? There was so much more that I wanted to accomplish. I wasn't ready for the year to be finished. Had I done enough? Had I tried to do too much? As I asked myself these questions, I realized that I was asking the questions too late. I should have *started* the year by asking myself core questions about my practice and curriculum. More than 20 years later, I still carry the lessons of that first June. I know that I haven't seen it all, and I certainly don't know it all. But now I am more deliberate about making every year count.

A good friend often talks to his staff about how lucky we are as educators because we have a start and finish every year. At the end of the year, we get time to reflect and make plans for the next year. What a powerful time it is: springboard from a great year to a better one or, if it was a year marked by difficulty, learn from the year and then put it in the past.

**The bigger picture.** An emotional stop and start motivates me each year. But I always tend to look at each year as a discrete time period. This year is over; next year, I'll do this or that. I rarely look at longer chunks of time. Recently a book title caught my eye: *Where Will You Be Five Years from Today?* The title reminded me of a question I had asked many times in job interviews. It made me think about my students, too. Where did I want them to be in five years? Have I done what it takes to help them get where they need to be in five years?

**Where will you be?** Very simply, the book encourages each reader to plan the next five years of their lives. The author gives some examples of what can be accomplished in five short years. Michelangelo painted the Sistine Chapel in fewer than five years. Shakespeare wrote *Hamlet, Othello, King Lear, Macbeth,* and five other plays in fewer than five years. Though I could never paint the Sistine Chapel or write like Shakespeare, I know that I can accomplish a number of things in the next five years if I set goals and create a plan—if I look for opportunities rather than focus on roadblocks. The book encourages readers to live life with purpose. So, I pose these two questions to you: What is your purpose? What do you want your students' purposes to be? Whether you are a teacher or administrator, think about what your life's work is. Then break your life's purpose down to the next five years.

**What is your purpose?** I am not encouraging you to set unattainable goals. Instead I ask you, this year did you live your life with purpose? Did you help your students live each day with purpose? Did you help your colleagues live each day with purpose? Five years from today, what do you want to look back at with satisfaction? As educators, we are used to thinking about years. Our lives have been nicely chunked into year-long slots that have a beginning and end. But we rarely think of a long-term goal, or a project that can take several years to accomplish. When I began to think this way, five years seemed like a long time, but it can certainly pass by very fast.

**What do you want your students' purpose to be?** As middle grades educators, I want you to think about where your students will be five years from now. If you teach fifth graders, those students will be in high school within five years. If you teach eighth graders, those students will have graduated from high school. Where do you want your students to be five years from now? Did you do enough to help them get there? Begin to think of your students not as fifth, sixth, seventh, or eighth graders, but as middle grades students. As you think this way, you will begin to develop a vision for where you want your students to be five years from now.

We tend to do a good job thinking of individual curricula with a long-term view. For example, a fifth grade social studies teacher probably has a good idea where his or her students should be when they study social studies as a tenth grader. However, do we think about the whole child and where they will be five years from now? What types of skills should we help them develop? What can we do to encourage them to be creative thinkers? How can we teach them to be responsible citizens?

One of our country's greatest leaders was Abraham Lincoln. He had a vision of the country that he was willing to risk his political career on. He once said "And in the end, it's not the years in your life that count. It's the life in your years." Let's make sure that from now on, we make each year count, as well as each of the next five years.

---

## EXTENDING YOUR THINKING

- On the first day of the next school year when you meet with staff members, how will you communicate your purpose for the year? For the next five years?
- Create a timeline to plan your key leadership goals for the upcoming year, including attention to some of the unfinished business from last year. Be specific about the times.
- Create two lists of professional and leadership goals for yourself. One should encompass the next two years. The other list should include goals for years 3–5.

---

# Making a Place Where Each Student Belongs

How can we learn from what we have done? How is the experienced administrator or teacher different from the novice? How do we know what works? How can we get better?

Almost 20 years ago, I met one of the most extraordinary middle grades students I have ever known. I knew Justin primarily from coaching him in football, but I also had the pleasure of teaching him. By most ordinary measures, he was not remarkable—just an average student with average athletic ability and the typical social life of a young adolescent. Justin was the definition of a student in the middle.

But he also stood out a bit from his peers. He never missed school, had a very positive attitude, and always wore a smile. According to all of his teachers, he came to class prepared every single day. He always completed his homework and turned it in on time. On the football field, he practiced hard and worked to make himself better.

One day I learned what made Justin truly remarkable. For several weeks, he had been living by himself. We had known his mother was in jail but not that his father had been taken to a rehabilitation facility. This student cared for himself and came to school on his own each day. To feed himself, he earned money by carrying grocery bags out to shoppers' cars. He even spoke to bill collectors to get additional time to pay the bills. I've often wondered how a student like Justin was able to overcome all of the obstacles placed in front of him and still succeed at school when so many other middle level students need a major push just to come to school each day prepared to learn.

During this same time, I taught Chad, who was the complete opposite of Justin. Whereas Justin could make a day better because of his work ethic and attitude, Chad could make any day worse, sometimes without even trying. Rarely doing any work, he was one of those students who seemed to bring out the worst in his classmates. Knowing exactly where the line was, Chad crossed it every single day—and flaunted it.

As the year went on, he had bad days and worse days, but he was never absent. Like Justin, Chad had perfect attendance. Think back to those students whose absences you longed for; the students who drove you absolutely crazy and made those around them miserable. The students with the unique ability to find your last nerve, then stomp on it. Why is it those students are rarely absent from school?

Although at first glance, Chad and Justin seem completely different, closer examination reveals they have a core commonality. Such students are always at school because they need a place to belong. Your most difficult disciplinary case is the one who most needs the structure provided by your high expectations. The student with the most difficult home life needs your consistency and compassion. The toughest students in the classroom are the ones who most need to be there. When we accept the challenges the Justins and Chads of the world bring to our schools and strive to create an environment where each student belongs, we make a difference in the world.

Although students like Chad may frustrate us to the point of making us question our decision to work with middle grades students, we must provide them with the same things that we naturally give the less-needy students. If we make learning relevant for them, if we challenge them, and if we make learning exploratory in nature, we can make sure all of our Chads feel like they belong. Performing at a higher level and behaving appropriately are valid and attainable goals for this group of students.

**Letting go.** I recently heard a story about a way primitive hunters trap monkeys. Although monkeys are very intelligent, they fall for this simple trap. The hunter takes a coconut and drills a hole through the top. The hole is just large enough for a monkey to reach his paw into the hole. The hunter then attaches the coconut to a tree and puts some nuts and berries inside the coconut. When the monkey smells the nuts and berries inside the coconut, it tries to get them out by reaching inside. The monkey gets the berries, but he is unable to get his fist back out of the hole. He's trapped. Of course, all the monkey has to do to escape the trap is to let go of the nuts and berries. However, he wants to get the berries and nuts so much that the simple act of letting go does not occur to him and he remains trapped.

**We know what to do—we just don't do it.** Sometimes middle grades educators are like the monkey. We know what we ought to do, but we refuse to let go of something that we desire or think will work, even if letting go would be beneficial. We want to help all our students succeed, so sometimes we hold onto things that we have done in the past. Sometimes, even though we know what we should do to help students succeed, we cling to practices that were once successful or ones that we think would be successful. When we cling to a way of doing something that doesn't work, we act just like the monkeys.

**Developing authentic relationships.** We know what can motivate kids and what works best. We need to make sure that we take into account our experience and research of what effective middle grades practices are, such as making learning relevant and exciting while allowing students to feel part of a team, giving them a place to belong. Middle level education will always be about making connections with our students. When we are able to let go of practices we should release, we will be able to develop true, authentic relationships with students, thus leading to an environment where students are motivated to come to school because they know they are part of something special.

---

### EXTENDING YOUR THINKING

- What are some practices you use that you want to let go of? Create a list.
- Critically examine the list and make a commitment to what needs to stay and jettison what needs to go.
- What does the literature base say?
- What evidence do you have from your own practice about the effectiveness (or ineffectiveness) of some practices?

---

# Crafting a Vision for Change

How can school leaders understand the context of their situations? How do leaders start to craft a vision for systemic change? How do leaders differentiate between the effective and the ineffective?

Given the often-tumultuous nature of education, it is easy to become overwhelmed by all that goes on around us on a daily basis—some positive and some negative. Perspective allows us to maintain a balance, to remember that the grass is not always greener on the other side, and that in times of crisis, "this, too, shall pass."

Yes, it is easy to focus on the green grass in our neighbor's yard: a supportive administration, active parents, high-achieving students, a better view from the classroom window. However, focusing on the apparent good fortune of others can make us blind to the positive aspects of our own situation. We become convinced that we need to change aspects of our lives so we, too, can enjoy greener grass on our side of the fence. But when we look at our neighbor's yard—our colleagues' lives—what we are really seeing is patches of green. We may be missing the fact that those patches could be surrounded by dirt or weeds. It's easy to look at someone else and see all of the wonderful things he has; it's harder to distinguish the things that person may want to change.

**Having a healthy perspective.** We all can find at least one aspect of our job that we would like to change. It could be salary, class schedule, teaching assignment, or after-school responsibilities. That's where perspective comes in. When we start obsessing about the negative parts of our jobs, we need to step back and survey the scene. We might realize that we are actually standing on the most perfect patch of all. By having a healthy perspective about our jobs, we can make a more positive impact on student learning. I believe we can find many more pleasurable moments in life than negative ones, even though we may all have to deal with the death of loved ones, loss of a job, or financial crises. These realities sometimes make it hard for us to come to work ready to meet the daily challenges in the life of a middle grades educator.

One way I have dealt with life's challenges is by simply looking into the eyes of a child when I come to school. Not knowing what that child had to deal with prior to coming to school that morning helps provide the proper perspective for me to overcome whatever obstacles I will face.

Someone who serves as a model for this perspective is Mike Janatovich, a seventh grade science teacher with an infectious smile. I would challenge anybody to find Mike in a bad mood, depressed, or unhappy with his lot in life. Yes, he may argue for a different teaching assignment or wish he had more support from parents, but if he is not completely satisfied with all aspects of his career, you would never know it. He has a bright perspective that keeps him focused on his most important job: educating his students.

**Pursuit of happiness.** When people are happy doing what they are doing, they do it better. There may not be much research supporting that statement, but I would debate that point with anyone who might question it. Malcolm Gladwell wrote an essay, "The Pitchman," about Ron Popeil, the self-made billionaire and president of Ronco, producer of such household items as Veg-o-Matic, Dial-o-Matic, and Pocket Fisherman. Gladwell explains that there were many times in the beginning of Popeil's career when he may have looked at other patches of grass that he considered greener than his own. If he had opted to leave what he loved, in order to pursue other opportunities, he would never have been as successful as he was. Even through difficult times, he was not thrown off course by the brighter shades of green he saw other people standing on. He had perspective.

As we evaluate our lot in life, perspective will ultimately lead us to accomplish our goals. At the times when we are most challenged to find positives in our careers, we must remember to first look down and evaluate what we do have instead of focusing on what we don't have. By doing this one simple thing, we will have a much greater chance of keeping perspective and ultimately being happier with the patch of green we are standing on.

As renowned author Wayne Dyer so aptly says, "If you change the way you look at things, the things you look at change."

---

## EXTENDING YOUR THINKING

- What are five characteristics of your current situation that you would never trade? Why?
- Do you find yourself spending time and listening to people who tell you that things won't work? Listening to people who fixate on the problems, and are not focused on solutions?
- What are five things you can do right now to help others focus on solutions and not problems?
- What are five characteristics of your current situation that you could dispense with right now? Why these five?

---

# Leveraging Power to Effect Change

If no one leads, what happens? How do leaders leverage a variety of types of power to effect change? How do leaders take personal responsibility for dynamic change?

As I become energized for the new school year, I find myself evaluating middle grades practices in our district and across our state. And, although I have read the Association for Middle Level Education's groundbreaking publication *This We Believe* (2010) many times, I will review it again, as I do before every new school year. This annual re-reading keeps the most important concepts for middle grades students fresh in my mind.

This year, my perspective of *This We Believe* and my evaluation of what's going on in middle level education locally and nationally are colored by the country's economic climate, which puts financial strains on education in general and middle schools specifically. I am a firm believer in the importance of strong middle grades practices, and wonder if we, as middle grades educators, are advocating strongly enough to keep best practices in our schools. As educators, we need to be a strong voice to protect quality instruction in the face of pressure from outside groups.

There are countless examples of legislators and community leaders trying to dictate what we do. Unfunded mandates like *No Child Left Behind* and the *Individuals with Disabilities Education Improvement Act*, as well as poorly conceived high-stakes tests are a few good examples of the dangers of ceding control to political forces. It is time educators band together and become a strong, positive voice for middle grades education. If we fail to do so, middle grades practices that are critical to the healthy development of young adolescents will fade into oblivion. Ultimately, we will fall prey to the junior high mentality we have worked so hard to overcome and lose what is truly best for our students. To continue to serve our students well, we must publicize our successes not only in our district, but in state and national publications as well. We need to become our own cheerleaders.

**Defending middle grades practices.** Fallout of slashed budgets includes the financially motivated decision to move the middle grades into elementary or high school buildings. In these cases, middle grades practices may be lost in the shuffle. We must be strong advocates of maintaining the philosophy and best practices of middle level education for young adolescents even if the configuration of the building changes. Middle school is not about grade configuration; it's about ensuring young people have access to programs that, according to *This We Believe*, are

- Developmentally responsive
- Challenging
- Empowering
- Equitable

Practices that are critical in a successful middle school should not disappear if our schools change. The new organizational structure may not provide shared planning time or interdisciplinary units, so teachers and administrators must find a way to make them happen. If economic realities make best practices (such as shared planning time) things of the past, we still have an ethical obligation to do what is developmentally best for our students.

**Teaching the whole child.** Equally disturbing is the tendency— especially during hard economic times—to eliminate any programs that are not associated with mandated testing areas. Again, it is our duty to advocate for the best interests of our students. Young adolescents need the opportunity to develop their talents and experiment with subjects like art and music. They must develop healthy habits through physical education, health, and family and consumer science. There is much research to support the importance of these subjects, but the evidence is cast aside far too easily.

Although core academic areas will always be the focus of high-stakes testing, we must ensure a place for the arts, even if legislators largely ignore the student outcomes associated with them. As strong advocates, we can remind people outside education that it is impossible to measure everything of value on standardized tests. In fact, the increased emphasis on testing can deprive students of a high quality, well-rounded education. Some mandates also contradict what we know about learning styles and brain development.

Common assessments, which are developed collaboratively by teachers, have become a particularly good way to obtain data about student achievement. However, the data mined from common assessments sometimes paints an inaccurate portrait. We must keep the whole child in mind at all times, differentiating instruction and assessment as much as possible.

Similarly, we must ensure the elements of 21st century learning have a place in our education system. Our world is ever-changing and our students must understand and be prepared for the uniqueness of their future. Therefore, we must advocate for the 21st century skills outlined by the Partnership for 21st Century Skills, such as creativity and innovation, critical thinking and problem solving, communication and collaboration, information literacy, media literacy, information and communication technology literacy, and life and career skills.

**Step up now.** Remember, your ethical obligation as an educator is to do what is best for our nation's youth. If your teachers are hampered by pacing guides, common assessments, or lack of emphasis on 21st century skills, remember what makes your students tick. Students need to be active, purposeful learners; they need a challenging, relevant curriculum. Teachers need to address multiple learning styles and use a variety of assessment techniques.

Remember that young adolescents are at fragile points in their lives. Allow teachers time to work with the whole child. Fight to protect true middle grades schools and the practices that make them thrive. We have worked hard to help others understand the distinction and uniqueness of working with young adolescents. Do not be shy about trumpeting your successes in middle grades buildings. People in your community need to know the importance of middle grades education, as do your own district personnel.

As educators, we face many challenges every day as we work with students. If we continue to work hard and share our stories of success, we can make a difference in the lives of young adolescents. But we need to be willing to change. The time has come to be more aggressive in our advocacy for middle level education. We can wait no longer. In the absence of our action, others will continue to push their own agendas on our students. Be your own advocate. Be the students' advocate! After all, if not you, then who?

---

## EXTENDING YOUR THINKING

- Develop a presentation to share with colleagues, administrators, parents, or community members that highlights the unique gifts that middle level education provides to young adolescents.
- Read *This We Believe: Keys to Educating Young Adolescents* (2010), then write a letter to a principal or influential personnel in the district to encourage them to embrace many of the middle level principles outlined in the book.

---

# Lead by Motivating

What characteristics do inspiring leaders share? What can leaders learn from the past?

---

In his book *Drive: The Surprising Truth About What Motivates Us*, Daniel Pink says that intrinsic motivation is the key to a successful career. While much of the book deals with employers and employees, he draws similar conclusions about teachers and students. Pink writes about three levels of human motivation, which he calls Motivation 1.0, 2.0, and 3.0.

*Motivation 1.0* refers to early humans' simple need to survive. They were motivated to do whatever was necessary to maintain their existence. As society developed and cities began to emerge, so did *Motivation 2.0:* carrot or stick motivation. This concept involves encouraging and rewarding positive behaviors and discouraging inappropriate behaviors through punishment.

Most education systems are set up with the assumption that Motivation 2.0 is what drives students. There are countless examples of sticks: detentions, suspensions, and restricted participation in athletics and co-curricular activities. Examples of carrots include honor roll, student of the month, and the wide variety of classroom management schemes allowing students to earn rewards or privileges.

Carrots and sticks are extrinsic motivators—things we do *to* others to get them to work. However, extrinsic motivators do not always work with people. For example, Pink described a study of parental behavior at child care facilities that revealed that when a child care facility instituted a monetary penalty for late pick-ups, the number of late pickups skyrocketed. When the penalty for picking up children late was shame and embarrassment, few parents were late.

Pink's *Motivation 3.0* is intrinsic motivation. He says, "Human beings have an innate inner drive to be autonomous, self-determined, and connected to one another. And when that drive is liberated, people achieve more and live richer lives."

As the principal of Willowick Middle School 12 years ago, I tried to increase the number of donations to our canned food drive by offering incentives. I thought if we promised something extrinsic, like a pizza lunch, the donations would start pouring in. Much to my dismay, that was not the case. It wasn't until I reminded the students that the canned food drive would have a positive impact on the community did the donations increase significantly. Educators should not assume that we will see the most success when we reward students. Instead, our focus should be on making sure our students are intrinsically motivated.

**Lighting a fire.** Many of the concepts of effective middle grades education aim at developing the entire student. What can middle grades educators do to help make sure students are autonomous, self-determined, and connected to one another? How can we spark intrinsic motivation? First, take into account the personal experiences you have had with students. Have you gotten to know them through conversations and other informal means? If you haven't, take time to talk to students and, more important, listen to what they have to say.

Create surveys or questionnaires so you discover what they strive to become. Learn everything you can about their goals and then help them get there. Once you know your students well, you will know how to work on their intrinsic motivation. Next, look at students' assessment data. Most likely, the areas where your students have demonstrated strengths are areas in which they have developed interests. You are responsible for fostering their interests into a love of learning and a desire to learn all they can about those areas.

As principal, look at your teachers' practices. For example, Pink suggests teachers use a three-part test to see if homework is a positive force. For homework to help a student develop intrinsic motivation, teachers ask themselves whether they are "offering students autonomy over how and when to do this work." Next, they evaluate whether the assignment promotes "mastery by offering a novel, engaging task (as opposed to rote reformulation of something already covered in class)." Finally, they ask whether students understand the purpose of the assignment. If assignments do not pass all three parts of this test, teachers need to make modifications so that they do.

In addition, examine teachers' classroom management practices for evidence that they encourage students to make mature decisions. Were your students involved in developing the school and classroom rules? If the rules in the school are merely a collection of "sticks," change them so students begin to take more responsibility for their behavior. During the past 15 years I have never given a detention, a suspension, or a Saturday School assignment. In fact, I have never doled out a punishment. When most students hear this, they are puzzled; others are quite relieved to think they finally have an administrator who does not punish. Of course, poor decisions don't go unrecognized. When I talk with students I emphasize that they are ultimately responsible for those decisions and a consequence is given. After they leave my office, they are much more likely to take control of their actions in the future. This approach will not work 100% of the time, but you will be more successful if you focus on the students' decisions, not their behavior.

Another strategy to promote intrinsic motivation is to relate content to the world in which the students live. If they can see how the content affects them, they are more likely to learn it. In addition, subject matter should be relevant to the other material students are learning. Many middle schools have eliminated the barriers between subjects by creating interdisciplinary thematic units. Continue to do this, and students will be more involved in their own learning. As you encourage students to become or remain intrinsically motivated, you, too, will be recharged, more connected to the school, and motivated in your teaching. When your students are intrinsically motivated, your school and your classroom will become better places in which to work and learn.

We can take lessons from a leader who intrinsically motivated millions. Quoting the well-known leader Gandhi, let's all "Be the change we wish to see in the world."

## EXTENDING YOUR THINKING

- List three motivators in your life. What makes these your motivators?
- How can you maximize the effect of these motivators?
- How can you use them to power through the difficult times?
- When you decide to make a change, what factors trigger that change? Are they external or internal?
- To what degree does data play a role in your thoughts about change?

# Using the Data

How do schools decide what to do? How do schools decide
what works? What actually does work?

When people struggle to explain a complex situation, they often fall back
on a familiar phrase: "The devil's in the details." This common nugget
is a shorthand way of saying that if we don't pay attention to the minute
details when planning, we are not likely to be successful. Now, more than
ever, the details drive what we do on a daily basis. In Malcolm Gladwell's
book, *Outliers*, he writes about the complexity of flying a plane and the
importance of a pilot being detail-oriented. Gladwell describes a pilot who
made seven discrete errors that led to a plane crash. Avoiding even one of
the seven errors would have averted the tragedy.

In the field of education, the devil is actually in the *data*. Using required
tests to judge districts and schools means that we need to be clearly
focused on the meaning of the data and how we can use data to reach each
student. When we lose focus on the meaning of the data that is available
to us, we lose our education focus. A focus on data and its uses means
different things for different professionals in school settings.

**Data and building administrators.** Building administrators must be the
experts in data and be committed to doing whatever is necessary to learn
what data shows about classroom practice and student achievement. When
building administrators have a functional understanding of the available
data, they can use it more effectively. By giving teachers access to that
data, administrators and teachers can work together to produce positive
results. Often we think about using data solely to drive instruction. When
we fall prey to this mentality, we lose sight of the power of using data in all
aspects of leading a school or team.

When I was in my first year as a principal, I received many great tips and
much good advice. By far the best advice I received was from a survey
I did of the staff I was going to lead. After receiving a near perfect 98%

return rate, I reflected on the results. It was evident that the vast majority of the teachers wanted an inclusive middle school: a middle school that was responsive to the developmental needs of the young adolescents we served. We had many veteran teachers and several new teachers, so the school was primed for a major change. As we moved from a junior high to a developmentally-responsive middle school, I talked throughout the process about the survey results and what the data showed. The school became a much more inclusive learning environment that met more of our students' needs. Consequently, the students performed significantly better on state tests. This is one example of practical data use that resulted in functional transformation at the building level.

Too often, administrators hear the word "data" and think only of state test results and short-cycle assessments. Visionary leaders, at the middle level and elsewhere, must be willing and capable of using data in innovative ways to drive effectiveness. For example, if you want to change the way you report grades to parents, get data to help inform your decision. Survey parents to ask them how they would like grades reported. Survey other school districts to see how they report grades. Use the survey results to help determine how to change your grade reporting system.

Obviously, we have student data in the form of standardized testing. But we have other critical pieces of data that we use in a school. For example, how many parents attended parent/teacher conferences? Did they fill out a survey afterwards that helped you plan next year's conferences? Attendance data is important, too. Many states rate schools and use attendance as one of the criteria. Are there ways you can improve student attendance by looking at the data? Before implementing any new program, we must gather baseline data first, so we can later examine whether the program is effective.

**Data and classroom teachers.** Ensure that classroom teachers are familiar with all the available data about each student. Discuss the use of data with them. Ask teachers: What data are important? What do you do with the information you are given about your students? What extra data do you seek? What data do you collect through instruction and assessment for your own use? Do you use the data formatively (as a periodic measurement) to drive instruction?

Administrators need to be creative in making sure that teachers get time to work with other teachers to collaborate in assigning meaning to the data. Opportunities may come in the form of common planning time, staff development time, or time before the school year. As teachers work collaboratively to interpret data, they will gain the benefit of working with other people who perhaps see things differently and in whom they can develop a trust that allows sharing of personal data without fear of judgment or punishment.

Be certain teachers use the assessment data to meaningfully inform their instruction—that they use evaluation instruments that provide information they can use to compare students' strengths and weaknesses and that they then change instruction as needed. Stress that the data is for *understanding and driving instruction—not for placing blame.* It is critical to use data to find patterns of strengths and weaknesses in each student. Having data that are accurate and meaningful to all stakeholders is a key to an excellent middle school. As we continue to juggle our various daily responsibilities, it is critical that we use data to *help drive our educational practices.* After all, in the absence of data, all we have is opinion, and as we know, opinions can differ and can paralyze schools. Let's use the data to make the difference in meeting the needs of young adolescents.

---

## EXTENDING YOUR THINKING

- Do you have a system for collecting data in your school? If yes, how is it used to drive instruction and programming?
- Use a form of polling software to gauge how students feel about the school. Present your findings at a faculty meeting or lead a professional discussion.
- If you do not have such a system, develop one.
- Poll your staff about data use. Find out what they use and how they use it.
- Begin a conversation with teachers about how to increase effectiveness and efficiency of data usage.

---

. . . . . . . . . . . . . . . . . . . . . . . . .
TOPIC TWO
# IMPLEMENTING
. . . . . . . . . . . . . . . . . . . . . . . . .

## *Being There*

What can we learn by listening? How does a leader
decide when to stop thinking and start acting? What
are the characteristics of a good listener? How do those
characteristics overlap with traits of excellent leaders?

---

*"Are you going to be there?"* When I am asked this question I always smile, because it means that someone knows that I care. It might be a student-athlete asking about the game or a drama club member asking about opening night. Or it could be the orchestra member with an approaching concert. No matter what, the person asking hopes the answer is yes!

*Being there* is simultaneously the easiest and most complex part of our role as school administrators. Truly *being there* takes work, but when done effectively, it pays dividends that help kids. However, there is a cost to us as human beings who need to be somewhere else, too. The most pressing concern is our own immediate families. When our children are young, we need to spend time with them and bond. As they become older, they have activities that we enjoy attending. Those who have parents who also require care have another demand placed on them.

But the dividends of *being there* are many. For example, a friend of mine who is a high school principal diffused a situation that would have led to problems the next day by simply listening and checking into a possible problem at a weeknight basketball game. Rumors were circulating in the student community that afternoon, and when he heard students talking about a student making a hit-list of those he wanted to harm, the principal investigated the rumor thoroughly. He then was able to contact the offender's parents at home and avert any crisis that may have happened the next day. Though he missed most of the basketball game that night, my friend had a productive night.

**Being there for students.** *Being there* for students means both during and outside of the school day. Even though teachers monitor student behavior in the cafeteria, I try to spend some time there each day because students are less inhibited and more likely to talk if you meet them in a social situation. Your presence in the classrooms during the school day is important, too. Visiting their classrooms during the school day, you, as the administrator, send a message that you are an *instructional* leader who is following up on what is happening in the classroom—the most important part of their learning.

Although attending sporting events, concerts, and special events takes personal time out of your day, students want to see you and get to know you as a human being. Students look back at interactions at such events with fondness when, in later years, they reflect about their school careers. These are times when you can get more of "the whole child perspective" on students and be a role model to them.

**Being there for parents.** Parents also need to know you enjoy *being there*. Every time parents are in the building, I feel that I have an opportunity to develop positive relationships, so I never stay hidden in my office during events like parent/teacher conferences, open houses, or concerts. I value every opportunity to meet parents and show the positive things that are happening in the building. Whenever I have a microphone in my hands, I am acutely aware that I am sending each parent a message about their child's school.

Take time to create reasons for parents to come to school. Educational leaders often talk about the decline in parent involvement as students age from elementary to high school. But do we give them reasons to come to school? And when they do, do we take advantage of that time? Are conferences held during times that are conducive to busy schedules? Do we as administrators make an effort to get into the community to talk to parents?

**Being there for teachers.** How are you able to *be there* for teachers? The most difficult part for me is to make sure that I don't get trapped in my office. It is easy to claim that you have an open-door policy, but do you make an effort to visit your staff and see them in their classrooms? There are numerous ways to make sure you spend time in teachers' classrooms. Recently there has been a great deal of research into the effectiveness of walk-throughs. Whether structured and formal or more informal, the importance of walk-throughs in improving educational outcomes for students is clear: as educational leaders, if we take time to monitor instruction by being in the classroom every day, student learning improves.

It is also important to *be there* for your staff members outside of the school day. Much like I expect teachers to get to know their students and learn what motivates them, I get to know my staff members and become aware of what is happening in their lives. While it is important to maintain proper relationships, it is also important to know how the events happening in staff members' lives are affecting their work. Sick family members, impending major life decisions, and personal illness are all examples of situations that can affect staff members on a daily basis.

**Being there for colleagues.** We have an obligation to our profession to be there for each other. As budgets are cut and we are required to do more with less, it becomes easy to lose focus on our need to maintain professional contacts and help our profession grow. Administrators are prone to losing the feeling of human connectedness by virtue of the type of position they hold. Depending on the size of the building and district you work in, you may have some natural, non-supervisory relationships. However, upon leaving the ranks of teachers, you lose the natural support group of classroom teachers and become part of the "island" of administration.

How can an administrator remain connected to the "mainland" of our profession? I have a number of recommendations. First, stay current in research. Joining a group of educational colleagues gives you access to research and opportunities to develop yourself professionally. Attend conferences and workshops with the goal of developing a network of supportive colleagues while learning more about our great profession.

Second, develop proficiency in technology. As quickly as the landscape of technology changes, it will always be challenging to remain an expert. Think about technology systematically: Instead of spending hours playing and looking for the next big thing, pick an area that you are not familiar with and develop some expertise. For example, start with something as simple as Google docs or Moodle, programs that allow teachers to use technology to improve discussions, facilitate turning in assignments, and allow students to collaborate with each other.

Try following educational leaders who use Twitter to share research. After joining Twitter, find a way to avoid getting overwhelmed. Pick a time each day or evening to look at Twitter, mark articles or blogs that interest you, and systematically read and apply the information that you glean. Perhaps participate in an #edchat and develop a Professional Learning Network (PLN) to sharpen your skills and broaden your horizons.

**Wearing a myriad of hats.** Secondary administrators wear a myriad of hats. These include supervising teachers and non-teaching employees, being an instructional leader, planning professional development, managing extra-curricular activities, and being a spokesman for the profession of education. In any of these areas, it is easy to become overwhelmed at the prospect of continuing to run the daily operations of the school while simultaneously growing as a professional and dealing with the climate of change being driven by the current economy. I have, on a multitude of occasions, thought "it's not easy to be me." I wondered whether anyone else understood the challenges that I faced on a daily basis.

By becoming active in state and national organizations, I learned that there were other people who go through the same daily challenges as I do, and I have developed friendships with people throughout the country. I enjoy getting a phone call from a colleague in a different part of the country who is facing the same problem as I am or who wants some input into how to make a new program work.

But do not get bogged down. If you are spending all of your time looking for the next big idea, you are not developing and maintaining the relationships you need to have with your students, parents, and teachers. One friend went through a phase where he felt so overwhelmed by all the changes he needed to make, he stayed in his office for several weeks on end, working hard on planning the things he needed to do. As we talked, he realized that by secluding himself he was doing more harm than good to his psyche. He made a conscientious decision to spend more time in classrooms and with students, and his perspective changed back to one that was positive, leading him to become more productive again.

---

## EXTENDING YOUR THINKING

- Identify a group of stakeholders in your building or district for whom you have not been sufficiently "there."

- Identify ways that you could reach out to this group to maximize your relationship. In other words, how could you be a more useful presence for this group.

- Reflect on how increased engagement with this group could positively impact student outcomes in your building or district. Following your identification and reflection, get out of the office and start *being there!*

---

# Instructional Practices

What instructional practices provide the biggest impact on student achievement? What can leaders do to help teachers engage students? What can we learn from the Iceman?

Mr. Roach, "The Iceman," was well ahead of his time. His approach to education started and ended with building relationships. He was playful and seemed to have a personal relationship with each student he taught. Any of his former students at what is now Monticello Middle School in Ohio would agree that he was an unforgettable educator. Teaching a class that some would consider mundane at best—civics—he talked with excitement about the formation of government, the necessity of taxes, and the most practical of lessons: how to fill out the 1040 tax form. Mr. Roach could make you believe that everything he said was invaluable to your development as a student and a person as he made civics come alive.

Close to 30 years ago, he walked the halls with a stern look and a huge heart. He would encourage students to hurry to their next class with a "Better get going; The Iceman is here." His personality was much bigger than his physical stature (he was 5'3"), so he didn't intimidate middle grades students by his physical presence. However, reminiscent of the old E. F. Hutton commercials, when he spoke, you listened. Demonstrating his ability to relate to students the first day they were in his class, he laughingly introduced himself as The Iceman. Even his hall pass was engraved with "Iceman." Although we weren't quite clear about the reasoning behind the nickname, it didn't matter. He was and will always be The Iceman.

As he talked about the facts of government he scoured the room asking questions, probing for more in-depth answers and thoughts, all the while praising students for their efforts. His standards were exceptionally high, yet we, his students, always tried to reach or exceed them. Even for an average student like me, nothing but the best was acceptable for Mr. Roach as he asked challenging questions to stretch our thinking. He made young people in his classes want to be better students and people. His energy never seemed to subside, which to us was remarkable because he seemed to be about 105 years old (in retrospect, he was probably in his late 40s or early 50s).

**Beyond relationships.** At a time when the focus in education seems to be on everything else, we can all learn something from The Iceman. One of the most important qualities of an educator is the ability to connect with students and build relationships. When a teacher has a trusting relationship with students, learning takes on greater meaning. I can still remember some of the lessons Mr. Roach taught and that's probably because he clearly cared about us.

Let's not forgot the importance of relationships as we scour through test results to attach a number from a state mandated test to each individual student. While accountability and assessment are critical for schools to move forward, I don't ever want us to stop talking about the necessary nature of personal relationships with students. This is particularly true today, when more students seem to be struggling with balancing relationships with their friends and family. As the old adage goes, "Students don't care how much you know until they know how much you care."

I want to be perfectly clear; being an educator requires more than being a nice person who gets along with everyone. We need to:

> *Provide learning experiences that are relevant.* As far back as the 1700s in the United States, our colonies were focusing on classical instruction; the need for "useful knowledge" was stressed, according to scholar Meyer Reinhold. While some aspects of our education history may seem a bit archaic, useful knowledge is and always will be timely.

> *Challenge all students to reach their highest levels of performance.* We know that each student is unique but we continue to gear many of our instructional practices to students of average ability. Though it is much easier said than done, we have to focus our instruction on reaching and challenging all learners every day.

Plug "differentiation" into any search window for some great ideas to reach all students.

*Possess great content knowledge.* Samuel Johnson wrote: "Knowledge is of two kinds. We know a subject ourselves, or we know where we can find information on it." Not only do we need to have great content knowledge that we can use to capitalize on during teachable moments that arise, but we also must know where we can find additional information that will stretch all students' abilities.

*Use instructional methodologies that are based on best practices.* Each day is different, each class is unique, and all students are special. As we plan lessons, we must keep in mind what will most benefit our students at this particular moment in time (it might not be the lesson we used at this point previously). Using best practices that are evidence-based—modified to fit our classrooms—will lead us to greater achievement.

*Be creative and innovative as we plan for and implement our lessons.* Daniel Pink, author of the bestselling book *A Whole New Mind*, writes about the right and left hemispheres of the brain and the implications that new research has made for the future. Pink foresees the right side, which rules creativity and innovation, driving the future rather than the logical left side that is critical and analytical. While he recognizes the importance of both hemispheres working together, the right side is driving what Pink describes as the Conceptual Age. He notes, "With facts easily accessible to us all, each one becomes less valuable. What begins to matter more is the ability to place these facts in context and deliver them with emotional impact."

**The Iceman's legacy.** My sister, Sally Burton, is an amazing teacher with a remarkable ability to connect with her students. Because I live in the community where she teaches, I hear stories about her all the time. "Ms. B. is amazing." "I loved her class." When I ask her students both present and past what makes her class so good, the answers seem to come out in identical statements. "She makes learning fun." "It seems like she knows everything." "Our lessons are exciting." "She spent extra time helping me." Not surprisingly, she was a student of the famed Mr. Roach. How many others must he have influenced, without even knowing it? A great teacher's impact can be felt for years, decades, and generations to come.

As we move forward in education, seeking to provide a greater education experience in the global society for our students, remember that your greatest asset is the person who looks back at you in the mirror. Undoubtedly, The Iceman could look in the mirror with confidence to know that he was being true to his students in the relationships he built. To paraphrase the great Ralph Waldo Emerson, trust your students and they will be true to you; treat them great and they will show themselves to be great.

---

## EXTENDING YOUR THINKING

- Who is someone in your school setting who most clearly possesses the ability to reach all students with passion and purpose while maintaining trusting relationships?
- What, specifically, does this educator do to be successful with students?
- What are two characteristics or practices the educator uses that you should implement?

---

# Pillars of Character

What does it mean to be a good citizen? What does it mean to have strong character? Are there ways that schools can promote citizenship and character? How can we measure the effectiveness of school-based efforts to promote citizenship and character?

As we focus on data-driven decision making and preparing students for testing, we must not lose sight of the importance of teaching our students to be people of character. According to the Josephson Institute Center for Youth Ethics (http://josephsoninstitute.org), there are six qualities that we need to instill in our middle grades students to help them become the best people they can be. Those six pillars of character are trustworthiness, respect, responsibility, fairness, caring, and citizenship. We know it is not enough to tell students how important something is—we must show them as well. We do that by living these six traits every day.

For example, the Josephson Institute's description of *respect* includes "Deal peacefully with anger, insults, and disagreements." How do you show your students that you live your life with respect? When you disagree with a colleague, do you remain calm as you advocate for what you think is right? When a student makes an inappropriate comment, do you confront the student calmly and in a positive way?

You must show your *trustworthiness*—being reliable and doing what you say you'll do. If you tell the students you will make time to talk with them the next day, do you follow through? If you agree to help a struggling teacher after school, you must do it.

**Caring.** I'll never forget witnessing an unbelievable moment that demonstrated the characteristic of caring. At the 2012 Ohio track and field state championships I sat in the stands and intently watched the 3,200-meter run, a race that is long and physically taxing, especially in warm weather. Although earlier in the day Meghan Vogel had won the 1,600-meter run, she was in last place on the last lap. The runner in front of her collapsed. When the runner collapsed, Meghan was required by the rule of the sport to go around her competitor and continue with the race. If she helped the fallen athlete, she would be disqualified.

Yet when Meghan saw her competitor go down, she did not think about rules or golden opportunities to finish one place higher. Instead, she stopped and helped her competitor limp to the finish line, and then pushed her over it, meaning that she, herself, would finish in last place—that is, unless she was disqualified. The crowd cheered wildly for this high school student as she demonstrated the caring all educators hope to instill in their students. Fortunately, the officials recognized the stellar act of sportsmanship and did not disqualify her. After the race she told a newspaper reporter, "Helping her across the finish line was a lot more satisfying than winning the state championship."

A video of the final moments of the race went viral on the Internet, and the story took on a life of its own. Meghan not only pulled her competitor across the line, she pushed her ahead. As middle grades educators, we give our time to help our students. We hope to push them in front of us so they can reach further than they think they are able—further than we can take them.

**Be the safety gear.** Kathy Hunt-Ullock, a former advocate for middle grades students, often referred to them as "the whitewater in the river of life." As you work with your students this year, remember that as middle grades educators, you must be the young adolescents' safety gear during these often unsettled times—their lifejacket and helmet. You also can help them by teaching and living the six pillars of character.

---

### EXTENDING YOUR THINKING

- Perform five Random Acts of Kindness around your school.
- Pay close attention to see if your acts of kindness have led to others performing their own kind acts toward others.
- If the kind acts build their own momentum, you have two choices: reveal what you have done and any impact these acts may have had, or don't reveal what you have done and examine whether there is a long-term change in school culture.

---

# *Value of Diversity*

How can we best prepare students for the diverse and
inclusive world they will enter after they leave school?
Are there ways to infuse our curricula with meaningful
acknowledgements of the value of diversity?

As middle grades educators, we are all challenged to help our students
see the world outside the school, especially the wonderful richness that
its diversity can bring to their lives beyond the classroom. Some students
struggle to form positive relationships with students from different
backgrounds or beliefs than their own; others are eager to expand their
horizons. Regardless, all students can benefit from direct instruction about
the value of diversity.

When I was a middle grades teacher, I made a conscious effort to teach
about the richness of diversity. Almost without exception, every student
embraced the lesson, whether it was a classroom activity, assembly, or
other resource. Listening to students talk about the value of diversity
during and after school validated for me the importance of these lessons.

For one such lesson, I taught a poem called *The Cold Within*, by James Patrick
Kinney (see page 34). Before reading the poem as a class, I divided the
students into small groups and assigned each group a stanza. Students were
to read the stanza, write down what they interpreted as the meaning of the
stanza, discuss it as a group, and prepare a brief statement about the stanza.

Some stanzas were easy for students to interpret as outright racism or
religious bigotry. Other stanzas required more discussion and insight,
particularly those that addressed poverty. After each group had presented
its interpretation, I read the entire poem. I explained that I had not let
them see the entire poem before they did their group work because in life
we often jump to conclusions based on a narrow picture of something or
someone. We all judge people by the way they look, talk, by the clothes
they wear, and so forth. I wanted to see what questions the students would
ask and how they would explain the stanza outside of the entire poem.

I asked the students one follow up question. "Wasn't it easier to understand *The Cold Within* after hearing the complete poem?" Of course the answer was easy: "Yes." This lesson helped the students ask critical questions not just about the stanza and ultimately the poem, but also about the members of their group and about themselves. During the next several months, I noticed a difference among the students. Although they still got angry and struggled with relationships, they asked clarifying questions and tried to see the other person's point of view. Because it is critical to revisit lessons to ensure the message is sustained, I often referred to the lessons in the poem.

**Lesson in caring.** One of the most frustrating things we do as a society, in my opinion, is dedicate a month to recognizing a culture. My point is quite simple: we should recognize all cultures every day. It doesn't make sense to wait until a certain month before we celebrate the contributions, advancement, and history of a culture. Almost 14 years ago I learned about a character education program called Project Wisdom. The program encourages students to think about choices they make every day, and how these choices affect those around them. One component of the program is a daily message that is meant to teach about character. At the end of the message, the narrator says, "Make it a great day… or not. The choice is yours."

One of the things I appreciate most about these daily messages is that the messages are from people of diverse cultures. I believe that using these messages helps reinforce our need to respect different cultures each day, not just for a month. It is difficult to tackle topics such as racism, religious bigotry, and economic inequality with students. However, most students probably have already dealt with these issues in their lives. The poem, *The Cold Within*, is an excellent tool to teach students about character. I also believe we can empower students to deal with these issues if we give them a chance to learn about them as young adolescents. We hope they will learn that the choices they make every day affect those around them.

Helping students be kind, caring, open-minded thinkers is but one of our many jobs. Take the time to show examples of both right and wrong while capitalizing on those teachable moments. After all, it is always our choice to "make it a great day... or not." Let's help students make it a great one!

### The Cold Within

*By James Patrick Kinney*

Six humans trapped by happenstance
In bleak and bitter cold;
Each one possessed a stick of wood,
Or so the story's told.
Their dying fire in need of logs,
The first woman held hers back,
For on the faces around the fire,
She noticed one was black.
The next man looking cross the way,
Saw one not of his church,
And couldn't bring himself to give
The fire his stick of birch.
The third one sat in tattered clothes,
He gave his coat a hitch.
Why should his log be put to use,
To warm the idle rich?
The rich man just sat back and thought
Of the wealth he had in store.
And how to keep what he had earned
From the lazy, shiftless poor.
The black man's face bespoke revenge
As the fire passed from his sight,
For all he saw in his stick of wood
Was a chance to spite the white.
The last man of this forlorn group
Did naught except for gain
Giving only to those who gave
Was how he played the game.
Their logs held tight in death's still hand

Was proof of human sin.

They didn't die from the cold without,

They died from the cold within.

## EXTENDING YOUR THINKING

- At the start of the year, take time in a faculty or team meeting to have teachers write down an experience in their teaching career when students had "aha" moments about the value of diversity. Put all the responses in a hat. Shake the hat and draw three to read at the start of each meeting throughout the year.

- What character traits does your school teach to students? How were they selected? How are they modeled by the adults in the community? How are they celebrated?

- Does your school community prioritize teaching students to make good decisions? How do students know it is a priority?

# *Student Leadership*

Developing leaders one student at a time—why? What is the capacity of your school to develop leadership throughout your school?

In the close to 20 years since I earned my master's degree, I've considered leadership and its implications more than most other educational topics. What is leadership? What attributes do leaders share? How can leaders be developed? My answers to those questions have gone through myriad permutations as I have grown as an individual and as an educator. In the spirit of that internal dialogue, I'd like you to step away from this chapter for a moment and define leadership for yourself; this exercise will give the rest of this discussion some personal context.

Now that you have a brief definition, I wonder if it included a person such as Abraham Lincoln, Barack Obama, or perhaps a coach or athlete. I believe that leadership is much easier to point out in others than to define. When trying to define leadership, we often refer to characteristics that leaders possess and examples from our own experiences.

Instead of saying that leadership requires strength of character, we point to Abraham Lincoln, who displayed a great deal of character in reaching out to those who opposed him. Instead of saying that leadership involves inspiring others, we think of Barack Obama inspiring millions of people through his message of hope and change. Instead of saying that leadership means doing the right thing, we remember Dr. Martin Luther King, Jr., standing up in the face of injustice and leading with his heart, head, and with a message of nonviolence. If our ability to perceive and define leadership is firmly couched in our perception of individuals with leadership traits, we have an inherent responsibility to craft more leaders. If, as educators, we cannot define leadership without leaders, we need to provide similar exemplars to our students.

**What leadership is about.** One of the most important jobs we have as educators is to teach leadership skills to individuals and groups. We must help the young adolescents in our schools understand what leadership is all about. After all, we don't automatically expect our students to make good decisions, help others, show compassion, and be critical thinkers without some sort of formal instruction from us. They need similar instruction and support to become leaders.

Regardless of the grade configuration of your school or number of students in your building, please ensure that your students have the opportunity to participate in leadership training, whether it's through a structured advisory program or stand-alone initiative.

Fostering leadership has many positive effects. Helping students develop leadership skills helps them monitor their own and other students' decision-making ability, which ultimately leads to better academic performance and fewer negative behaviors. Our society is at a crossroads; with a struggling economy we need to ensure that our students will be prepared for the radical shifts of the 21st century. The students who have leadership skills will be able to weather the ups and downs and ultimately help others through the process.

It was glaringly apparent to me—as a new principal—that I needed to spend time helping my students develop leadership skills because we had far too many suspensions, and too few students were performing to their ability. Together with my assistant principal, I decided to talk to students to determine how we could help them develop better decision-making skills. The students were excited about our conversations and wanted to know if we could talk more. We decided to establish a leadership council. Every two weeks, I met with the student council officers and a couple of other students. During each meeting, we talked about various school issues as well as a large activity that would help our student body learn more about leadership. We discussed famous people and identified the characteristics that great leaders possess. The kids responded very well to the leadership council and the responsibilities they assumed. I have since changed jobs, but I never stopped having a leadership council. Having a leadership council has afforded me wonderful opportunities to work collaboratively with students, helping them organize and plan activities for the betterment of all students. One activity that has become a staple of the leadership council is the leadership lock-in.

**Leadership lock-in.** Leadership lock-in is an overnight program during which students participate in a variety of initiatives focused on leadership skills. The lock-in is open to all seventh and eighth graders; however, when I was working at a large middle school, we had to limit the number of students participating. Last year, 105 students attended and 30 former leadership council students helped with the program. Additionally, 15 parent volunteers helped in many different capacities, including the all-important nighttime supervision. While the lock-in was established to help all students develop leadership skills, it also gives the leadership council members an opportunity to expand their leadership skills by planning and leading students through activities. Furthermore, it gives past leadership council members the opportunity to run various initiatives. This overnight program has helped more than 1,000 students get a better grasp of leadership through teambuilding and decision-making activities.

The lock-in begins with a high-energy ice breaker facilitated by the current leadership council. The students break into as many as 10 groups (using communication skills) that remain together throughout the lock-in. Each team chooses its team name, chant, and quote, then reports to the larger group. After a brief discussion about leadership, the students get settled for the evening, report back for dinner, and review the agenda. After each activity students are required to make a journal entry detailing their experience. Some of the activities are:

> *Leadership 2 x 4.* Within each team, the students are divided into two teams. Each team faces the challenge of moving from one side of the cafeteria to the other using only 2 x 4 boards and a series of ropes that are attached through the center of each board. Communication skills are a key and after much problem solving, the students always find a way.

*Mission Leadership.* Each team determines the most important supplies to keep on a desert island. First, the students rank the items individually and then as a group. The discussions that follow are quite interesting as the teams try to reach consensus.

*Survival of the Fittest.* The teams are faced with many physical challenges that require teamwork to complete. The tasks are impossible without involving everyone on the team.

*Leadertech.* Each team quickly researches famous leaders and completes a digital visual presentation or a podcast about the attributes of the leader they chose.

After going through eight 30-minute leadership activities, the students get some free time and end the evening with a movie that focuses on one or many aspects of leadership. Some of the movies we have seen are *The Ultimate Gift, Pay It Forward,* and *School of Life.* After the movie, the students go to their sleeping areas to "try" to get some sleep.

After the students wake up, usually to some bad singing on the PA, we have a leadership craft activity, conduct one large group activity, and take some time to complete journals. Prior to leaving, we review the lock-in experience and talk about the future.

Without exception, the lock-in has been a hit wherever I've used it. This initiative has helped decrease referrals, detentions, and disciplinary infractions. The students love the experience and talk about it for years after. Whether it is a lock-in or some other type of leadership experience, helping students developing leadership skills will increase their desire to work harder and ultimately increase academic performance.

**Hands-on leadership.** I remember my father, a former history teacher with a great memory, talking about leadership and what it takes to be a leader. Often, he would quote famous leaders and ask me who he was quoting. It seemed he knew a quote from every major or minor historical figure. His favorite quote has quickly become mine. It is taken from a speech given by Theodore Roosevelt in the Sorbonne, Paris, almost 100 years ago:

It is not the critic who counts: not the man who points out how the strong man or where the doer of deeds could have done better. The credit belongs to the man who is actually in the arena, whose face is marred by dust and sweat and blood, who strives valiantly, who errs and comes up short again and again, because there is no effort without error or shortcoming, but who knows the great enthusiasms, the great devotions, who spends himself for a worthy cause; who, at the best, knows, in the end, the triumph of high achievement, and who, at the worst, if he fails, at least he fails while daring greatly, so that his place shall never be with those cold and timid souls who knew neither victory nor defeat.

Finally, I'll leave you with my own hard-earned definition of leadership. Leadership, quite simply, is the art of leading others to achieve. It is about being in the trenches, working hand-in-hand with others for the greater good. It is time for all middle level schools to give students opportunities to be in the leadership arena, so that they will "never be with those cold and timid souls who know neither victory nor defeat."

---

## EXTENDING YOUR THINKING

- Interview a respected student, teacher, and administrative leader in your own school setting to explore their perspectives on what leadership is. Make the leader define it.
- Ask each what he/she does to develop leadership.
- Interview a small group of students and staff. Ask them about the person you interviewed above. How does your small group see the person?
- What can their perspectives tell you about leadership?

---

# *Setting the Pace*

How fast is too fast? Who sets the pace? How can the wrong pace make problems worse? How can the right pace facilitate meaningful change?

Leading a middle school through a school year is much like preparing for a race—before it begins you are filled with questions about how the year will unfold—am I ready for the challenges, both known and unknown that I will face throughout the year? Like running a cross-country race, you head into a school year with a fast start, settle into a good pace, face a few challenges, and finish quickly. I offer here a walkthrough of snippets from my cross-country experience, blended with their application to middle level education.

**The First Leg:** *More than 200 runners were preparing to make their mark at the first cross-country meet of the year. I was not a gifted runner and knew that I would not be competitive in a big race. Once the starter raised the pistol, I was on my mark. For that moment, the silence was deafening; I couldn't hear anyone breathing. As the sound of the starter pistol echoed through the valley, I took off, sprinting to the turn. After all, my coach always said that we should start fast, settle into a good pace, and save a little extra for the end.*

> *Lesson:* Pace yourself. While the start of each year is exciting and is most often met with great enthusiasm, setting goals and having specific action steps for any new initiative will help you stay focused for the year. As a runner, I had to find the balance between falling behind and burning out. The same is true in education.
>
> Further, my relationship to other runners was secondary to my internal struggle to do my best. There will always be a faster runner, just as there will always be another school or district with better resources. An educator's ability to be the best teacher possible is a critical part of pacing; the goal is not to finish first, but to set a personal best.

**The Second Leg:** *I turned a corner and saw a very steep hill rising out of a field of weeds. As I followed the dusty path and the runners who were ahead of me, I knew my toughest battles were yet to come. Being behind and knowing that I had the majority of the race ahead of me was one thing, but I was just trying to survive and move up a few places. As I got closer to the hill, I realized that some of the runners had slowed considerably. I thought if I attacked the hill and kept moving, I could make up some time. After a few strides up the hill, I realized reaching my goal was going to be harder than I thought. It seemed easy enough. I was in good enough shape, had run hills before, and had an excellent coach. However, the incline was steep and the wind, which had been non-existent all day, seemed to pick up as I started my ascent.*

> *Lesson:* Plan for the hills and don't quit. Throughout the year, you will be faced with incredible challenges that in some cases will seem insurmountable. Overcoming an obstacle will take extra work and a focused determination. Dealing with difficult situations is never easy. Part of overcoming an obstacle is gathering information and separating the critical from the superfluous, the helpful from the damaging. Whether the obstacle is a difficult parent, implementation of a new program, a particularly challenging class, or some other unforeseen barrier to optimum practice, seeking assistance, maintaining focus, and pushing through to a positive solution are critical. You can't finish the race without getting over the hill.

**The Third Leg:** *As I reached the top and took my last step on the hill, I was relieved and relaxed. Just then, I heard my coach encouraging me to "push off the hill." He wanted me to continue to work hard after I made it up and over the hill. I quickened my pace and immediately understood why he encouraged me to do so. Some of the runners were walking after they made it up the hill, while others were barely jogging. It's easy to forget that the race is not over when the first obstacle is overcome; my coach reminded me that, while I had accomplished something, I was not yet finished.*

*Lesson:* Push off the hill and keep the momentum. After dealing with a difficult situation or implementing a program, maintain focus to ensure the situation is resolved or the program is running smoothly. When facing uphill battles, it is critical to continue moving in a positive direction. Far too often, educators abandon a practice or a program that is great for kids because a few vocal parents don't see the big picture. Todd Whitaker, author of *Dealing with Difficult Parents,* talks about one of the worst educational practices we have: allowing negative, non-supportive people to influence the decisions we make. As my coach encouraged me to do, you must maintain focus and momentum after reaching a goal.

**The Fourth Leg:** *After following my coach's advice and pushing off the hill, I saw the broad expanse of the rest of the race course in front of me. While I had just finished a difficult task and continued to work hard after its completion, I now saw that I wasn't all that close to the finish line; I had to keep running, uncertain if there were more hills or uninterrupted flat land in front of me.*

*The majority of the remainder of the race was relatively uneventful: a few rolling hills, a gentle stream, and a winding path through the woods. Coming out of the woods, I saw the finish line roughly a quarter of a mile away. I picked up my pace; I knew I must finish strong. As I crossed the finish line somewhere in the middle of the runners, I knew I had given it my all and would take this experience and learn from it.*

*Lesson:* Finish strong. As with any race, you must finish the school year strong. The school year passes in the blink of an eye, and before you know it, you are lined up again, ready for another school year, another race. Celebrating the success of the school year and the obstacles you've overcome is necessary and reassuring. You've completed a year with success; now you have to turn your attention, once again, to the next school year, as the process begins again.

**Getting back up.** At the end of last year, I was preparing my final thoughts to address students participating in eighth grade promotion, and I needed a little motivation which I got from a video aptly titled "Are You Going to Finish Strong?" In it, Nick Vujicic talks about finishing strong and getting up after falling down. Born with no arms or legs, he has the strength every day to get up if he falls down. Keep Nick in mind throughout the school year when it may seem difficult to continue to get back up after a difficult day, week, or even month; keep yourself inspired to focus on the kids, get up, and finish strong.

---

## EXTENDING YOUR THINKING

- One of the greatest challenges we have to overcome is striking the balance—achieving the perfect pace—to allow us flexibility to accomplish our goals. Look at the weekly calendar and write down the percentage of time at school you spend with students, staff, and paperwork (including data collection).
- Are the percentages in line with what you want? If not, how would you adjust them, and what needs to change to get there?
- Think about a colleague who is slow to embrace change. Think about a colleague who is eager to embrace new programs or practices. What can you learn from each?
- How can you strike a balance between going too slow and too fast?

---

## TOPIC THREE
# REFLECTING

# *Maintaining Momentum*

### Part 1 Sustaining Change

How do leaders and schools sustain change? How do schools continue to improve in the face of shifting objectives and conditions?

Like most people, I love magic. I love watching in awe as a magician disappears, narrowly escapes the "saw of death," or baffles me with a flying card. However, as we all know, the magician doesn't just disappear and the card can't possibly fly through the glass window. The illusions are incredible, but that's all they are: illusions. I believe that true magic happens each and every day in middle schools around the world. It is incumbent on all of us to help students learn new things, challenge students to reach levels previously unknown, light a fire within (as William Butler Yeats describes teaching), and recognize the true gifts of colleagues and students alike. Magic is what we believe to be possible, and I believe that by creating magical moments we leave behind a legacy that will make us proud. I also believe that there are six characteristics of great teachers that help create and sustain magical moments:

**1. Start with the end in mind.** Remember *Mr. Holland's Opus*? Mr. Holland didn't get into education to make a difference in the lives of his students. He was just passing time until he finished his opus. Every time I think about the movie, I laugh at the fact that he went into education because of the money. Although he never dreamed of such a long career in education, once he believed in his students, he focused on the end. He dreamed of great performances and worked to make that happen. Along the way, in a storied career, he left an indelible legacy. Great teachers start with the end in mind. After all, how do you know how to get there if you don't know where you are going? From the lessons we design to the games we coach and the activities we advise, we must always start with the end in mind.

**2. Focus on the solutions, not the problem.** Once we recognize a problem, we must devote our energy to finding a solution. Far too often, we are paralyzed by our problems. Hunter Campbell "Patch" Adams, M.D., whose story was told in the movie *Patch Adams*, was able to look past problems and focus on solutions. Because he was willing to look at alternative solutions, he often solved cases that had stumped his medical colleagues. Great school leaders find ways to help all students succeed. Patch Adams knew it; we should, too. The day-to-day grind can lead us down the path of negativity, especially if we don't feel supported or appreciated. However, staying positive and focusing on solutions puts us in a better place mentally and ultimately will lead us to a solution and perhaps a better workplace environment.

**3. Make the most of the time you have each and every day.** I didn't need the movie *School of Life* to remind me that life goes too fast. We lose family members, friends, and colleagues in the blink of an eye. However, the movie did drive home the point that we must use every minute of the day to reach students. Class periods, semesters, and school years go by much too fast. Yes, some years seem to drag on because of "that kid" or "that class," but just imagine the impact you might have had on those students had you been given more time.

As a young teacher I gave students a couple of free minutes at the end of each class because, I said, the class worked hard and it was only a couple of minutes. Yet by the end of the day or week I would yearn for more time, not realizing that I had all the time I needed. I just had to use the time wisely. We all need to use our time wisely. Plan accordingly and make the best use of the time every day. After all, once the clock stops ticking, we can't rewind it!

**4. Be able to shift and be innovative, yet stay on course.** The Emperor Penguins are a great example! In the movie *March of the Penguins*, we watch the incredible yearly journey of the Emperor Penguins as they make their way across the cold tundra of the South Pole. Even though the ice is constantly changing (reminds me of state and federal educational mandates) beneath the penguins' feet, they consistently reach their destination, time after time. Regardless of the roadblocks—and there are many—the penguins keep their eyes focused on the goal. One of my favorite quotes is "the only constant is change." With that in mind, we must always search for the best way to reach our students and be prepared to change quickly if we need to.

**5. Advocate for all students.** That means ALL students. In the movie *Radio*, an entire community rallied behind an intellectually disabled young man whom many believed didn't have a future or much of a life. But it took the efforts of an advocate, the head coach of a successful high school football team, who was willing to fight for what was right to bring the community together. Feeling guilty for the way his football players treated Radio, the coach invited him to help at practice and included Radio in team activities. Eventually, the team accepted Radio as part of the team although many community members and school employees believed he was a distraction. The coach held his ground, continuing to involve Radio in team activities and eventually resigning when the community refused to accept Radio. In an emotional good-bye, the coach reminded everyone that "we aren't the ones who've been teaching Radio. Radio was the one teaching us." As advocates for all students, we must stand strong and continue to push for what we know is best for our students. Regardless of ability and emotional level, all of our students need advocates. If we don't advocate for our students, who will?

**6. Leave a legacy.** You leave a legacy every day. The way you treat your students, colleagues, and parents will ultimately define your legacy. Your efforts can change the world. The movie *Pay It Forward* demonstrated how one assignment can, indeed, change the world.

**Hardly an illusion.** It is easy to lose focus and forget about the big picture as we face our daily challenges. When we are feeling down and perhaps question whether we are making a difference, we must start anew and be re-energized. We must remember that our students need our help, deserve our very best every day, and will flourish with our nurturing. Our job, quite frankly, never ends, and that is why it is daunting. However, we are rewarded every day as we see the connections being forged between students, between students and adults, and between students and content. As you attempt to balance an incredible work load, remember that we are paying it forward every day. When students see us helping others, they are more likely willing to lend a helping hand. Let's continue to create magic in the middle!

---

## EXTENDING YOUR THINKING

- Create a list of your greatest professional accomplishments of this past year.

- What legacy do you most want to leave your staff and students?

---

## Part 2  End-of-Year Refocus

What can teachers and leaders learn from the end of the
year? How can the end of the year inform the beginning of
the next?

At the end of each school year I take the better part of a weekend before
summer break to reflect. I always try to focus on the successes of the
past year but, like many other educators, my mind drifts to the things I
could have and should have done better. There's always a student ortwo
whom I could have done more to help or perhaps a program I could have
implemented more effectively. I reflect, take notes, and plan adjustments.
Five simple reminders help focus my thoughts and, ultimately, prepare for
the coming year:

**1. Each year provides a story or two.** Remember them and pass them on.
Without question, the story I will take with me this year is about Alyssa
Carnivale, an unbelievable young woman who stood in front of all the
other girls in the school and challenged them to be more tolerant and
understanding. At the end of the first semester, because of some unique
scheduling issues, students have some blocks of free time. Eighth grade
team leader Carolyn Douglas puts together activities for the girls and our
guidance counselor, Audrey Labenz, develops activities for the boys. This
year, the girls were challenged to come up with a commercial or skit to
help others get to know them better. Little did anyone know that a sixth
grade student would challenge everyone to look inside themselves and
value themselves and everyone else.

Alyssa is the type of student who comes to school every day ready and
willing to take on the responsibilities and opportunities it brings. Alyssa was
thrilled to share her thoughts, which ring as true today as they did earlier
in the school year: "Hello. I am Alyssa Carnivale. I am not exactly the same
as you. Sure, my hair doesn't go how I want it, but it is a beautiful shade
of brown. Yep, I'm not the best at sports, but I'm a great dancer who gets
good grades. Maybe I'm not the most popular girl at school, but I'm happy
because I have great friends. Sure, there are people who want to tear my

self-esteem down, but it's not happening because I'm happy being uniquely me. Here I am saying don't blend in because you're afraid you'll get teased. Yeah, I've been down that road and it's not fun, but if I learned anything, it's that we are all different and that is not going to change no matter how hard anyone tries. So, you might as well have fun being uniquely you!"

**2. Celebrate the successes of the year.** It is easy to focus on the things you wish you could do over. While I can easily fall into that trap, I make sure to note the positive things as well. This makes the successes more real and reminds me of the hard work and effort it took to accomplish them. Recognize the successes and celebrate them with your school community.

**3. Ask yourself what you would do differently.** Now you can write down the things you would have done differently. Make sure you focus on those things over which you have control. For example, one of the most frustrating aspects of education is the lack of parental support. While we can invite parents into the schools and explain the importance of being a team, in reality, parents must make the choice to be involved. Our parents of students at my school are supportive, but I know that parental involvement continues to frustrate many of my colleagues. After spending a great deal of time and resources, they are disappointed to have a large auditorium filled with only a handful of parents. I am not saying that we shouldn't try to encourage parent support or develop programs specifically for parents. Rather, we should not be too harsh on ourselves if they choose apathy over involvement.

Another area that always seems to be on my do-differently list is finding balance. I constantly struggle to find the right balance between office paperwork and classroom visits, work and home. At the end of every year, I tell myself that I am going to make changes next year so I can find that balance. While one may argue that educators can't achieve that balance because of constant interruptions and outside demands, I believe that if we make classroom visits or more home time a priority, we can make it happen. Therefore, this year I am making plans to be in the classrooms more next year, celebrating the inspiring lessons, encouraging students, and supporting teachers.

**4. Recognize that each student is unique, but patterns develop each year.** As we see our students develop in front of our eyes, we are reminded that each student is unique. However, as educators, we should take note of the individual class patterns and make plans for the future based on those patterns. For example, students may relish a specific project or assignment year after year. That tells us that the incoming classes will probably feel the same way. That project is a keeper. We must analyze what works in the classroom and in the school. Even though we all start with a clean slate in the fall, we should take advantage of what we know from the past.

**5. Create a stop-doing list.** Rather than a to-do list, I create a stop-doing list. I write down those things that I will stop doing or programs that I will stop supporting after I've evaluated them. As Dr. Marzano has mentioned in his writings, we must think like the gardener, eliminate the dying plants, and make room for the new growth. In education we spend a great deal of time developing new programs and working hard to implement them efficiently. However, we don't get rid of programs that aren't working. Thus, we continue to pile more work on top of a workload that is already incredibly demanding. Having a stop-doing list will allow for the space new plants and flowers or programs need to grow.

---

### EXTENDING YOUR THINKING

- At the start of the year, take time in a faculty or team meeting to have teachers write down a magical moment they have experienced in their teaching roles. Put all the responses in a hat. Shake the hat and draw three to read at the start of each meeting throughout the year.

- Create a list of unfinished business from the past year. Are there any items that could be deleted because they do not fit with your purpose? Which items must continue to be addressed until they are resolved?

- From what mistake or failure have you learned the most this year? How will it impact your leadership from now on?

---

## About the Author

Tom Burton has over 12 years' experience as a building principal and currently serves as the Director of Administrative Services in the Cuyahoga Heights School District, just outside Cleveland, Ohio. Now the Past-President of the Ohio Middle Level Association, Tom has also been a consultant for the Association for Middle Level Education (formerly NMSA). For the last 11 years, he has spoken to numerous audiences throughout the United States with passion and purpose on a multitude of topics. Additionally, Tom has written articles for publication including the "Mark of Leadership" column for *Middle Ground* magazine. He was a winner of the NASSP/MetLife Ohio Middle School Principal of the Year award and was selected as Ohio Educator of the Year by the Ohio Middle Level Association.

# About AMLE

Since its inception in 1973, the **Association for Middle Level Education** (AMLE) has been a voice for those committed to meeting the educational and developmental needs of young adolescents. AMLE is the only national education association dedicated exclusively to the growth of middle level education.

With more than 30,000 members representing principals, teachers, central office personnel, professors, college students, parents, community leaders, and educational consultants across the United States, Canada, and 46 other countries, AMLE welcomes and provides support to anyone interested in the health and education of young adolescents.

Through the release of our landmark position paper *This We Believe: Keys to Educating Young Adolescents*, AMLE has been a key resource to middle grades educators focused on developing more effective schools. Our message is for schools to be academically excellent, developmentally responsive, and socially equitable for every young adolescent. AMLE publishes *AMLE Magazine*, *Middle School Journal*, and *Research in Middle Level Education Online* to support members throughout the year, in addition to publishing books on a wide variety of middle level education topics. Our website, www.amle.org, provides a wealth of research and resources for educators, a complete online bookstore, and professional development event information. In addition to our annual conference, one of the largest professional development events in education today with nearly 6,000 attendees, AMLE offers a wide variety of more specialized professional development opportunities, including customized on-site professional development.

For more information about AMLE and our services, visit www.amle.org or call 1.800.528.6672.

CPSIA information can be obtained
at www.ICGtesting.com
Printed in the USA
FFOW05n2053171014